HUMAN CAPITAL
GROWTH MODEL

Build Best-in-Class Teams

(Second Edition)

ERIC ALAGAN

Disclaimer

Neither the author, the publisher nor distributor of this book shall have any liability to any person or entity with respect to any loss or damage caused or allegedly caused directly or indirectly from using the information contained in this book.

The Human Capital Growth Model (2nd Edition)

The second edition went through heavy revision. What little fluff existed in the original book was edited out and the page count reduced—without forsaking key content. In fact, this second edition contains 20 tables to the 10 in the first edition.

This book helps the reader to build a Human Capital Growth Model (HC Growth Model) in FIVE EASY STEPS.

The HC Growth Model allows you to:
1. Customise the model to your management style; your corporate values; and your current business cycle.
2. Identify and measure Human Capital in real numbers.
3. Compare apples to oranges and answer questions such as: Is your employee a 10 or a 7? Is your team a 9 or a 6.5?

This book is thin, and is thin on theory and specially designed for busy owners and managers of small and medium sized enterprises, and business units within larger corporations.

Note: Readers need no HR training to benefit from this book.

###

Table of Contents

Chapter 1: Three Types of Capital

You know people make the difference. But how do you take that great leap beyond cliché, from theory to hands-on application?

But first, some quick basics. Most managers and entrepreneurs are aware of the three types of capital required to provide products and services: financial, time, and human.

1.1 Financial Capital

Money grabs the most attention and the large corporations, with their deep pockets, enjoy a clear advantage.

1.2 Time Capital

Time is money. Unlike spent money, you cannot recover spent time. Moreover, everyone has the same 24 hours: an individual, a mom-and-pop shop or a huge corporation.

1.3 Human Capital

People working in an organization contribute their talent in exchange for rewards. But how do you measure the worth and value of their talent?

- Are employers hiring the right talents to the team?

- Are employers acquiring the right amount of talents to the team?

- How do you quantify talent? Can you quantify talent?

Yes, we can quantify talent but first we need to agree on what constitutes talent.

For our purposes, we refer to the term talent as all the human attributes required to achieve business success.

We condense that mouthful into one phrase: Human Capital.

1.3.1 Human Capital includes

- Hard skills (training and qualifications)

- Technical expertise (includes experience)

- Intangible qualities (soft skills)

Note: By soft skills we refer to diligence, integrity, and problem solving skills, and all the human attributes that fall in this genre— the elusive intangibles that differentiate winners from the herd.

As all businesses operate in teams, we need to look at individual human capital and team human capital.

1.3.2 This book will help you:

- Identify your employees' human capital i.e. Individual Human Capital (IHC)

- Build your team's human capital i.e. Team Human Capital (THC).

For convenience, throughout the book we use the phrase: human capital. Where it is important to differentiate between individual and team human capital, we shall indicate them as IHC or THC.

1.4 Key Takeaways from this book:

- How much human capital an employee possesses?

- How to identify and measure an individual's human capital (IHC) and your team's human capital (THC)?

- How to acquire and grow team human capital (THC)?

The good news: small and medium enterprises (SMEs) have a clear advantage when growing team human capital (THC).

The Human Capital Growth Model (we refer to it simply as the HC Growth Model) takes off from the Interview Stage.

In the next chapter, we shall briefly cover the steps leading to the actual interview. In essence, we shortlist candidates before the interview.

###

Chapter 2: Short List Candidates

Shortlisting candidates involves 3 steps:

- Define the Job Requirements
- Recruit a Pool of Candidates
- Short List the Candidates

2.1 Define the Job Requirements

The first step is for you to define your requirements regarding the job and the candidate:

- What is the job scope?
- What is the position you wish to fill?
- What skills do you seek in candidates?

This is usually handled by the human resource manager (HR manager) with input from the line manager who requested for the staff. If you own a small business, you might handle this.

Whether the new employee is a replacement staff or an addition to the head count, you probably follow the same process.

Let's assume you're seeking a sales person and these are the job scope and your requirements. See Table 1. Use a spreadsheet as it'll make your task easier.

Table 1: Job Scope and Requirements

Table 1: Sales Person	
Primary Job Scope	
1	Grow Existing Accounts
2	Prospect for New Accounts
3	Make Small Deliveries (upto 2 kg/parcel)
Requirements	
1	Minimum Diploma in Business/Sales/Engineering
2	Driver's License
3	Minimum 5 years in the Same/Related industry
4	Salary $5,000 per month, Commission, Benefits

It is quite common to see advertisements include <u>subjective</u> requirements such as:

We seek people who are:

- *Detail oriented*

- *Have a helicopter view*

- *Team players*

And so forth.

Nice touch but quite useless as every candidate thinks he fits the bill. Save the space. Save the money, as longer advertisements cost more. Stick to the essentials.

At the recruitment stage we keep to <u>objective</u> criteria.

- First, establish the job scope.

- Second, develop a list of objective job requirements that <u>match</u> the demands of the job scope.

In many small businesses, staff are expected to multitask. Therefore be transparent and include job scope details such as making deliveries and the parcel weight. These details would encourage women and older people, and even those with minor disabilities, to apply. It is morally right and also makes good business sense to practise an inclusive work environment.

Remember this: growing human capital starts with you. Grow your own individual human capital. You're the boss and there's no better leader than one who leads by example.

It's also good to indicate salaries as that helps sieve out job applicants. It would also attract candidates seeking wages higher than their current earnings and help widen the net. Some employers prefer to keep salaries confidential at this stage and only reveal it at interviews. Such an approach has its uses. Your call.

If you're handling the recruitment, come up with a score sheet to help shortlist the candidates. Assign a grade for each criteria. It's purely arbitrary but very helpful as you'll discover.

Once you set the grades, your assistant can quickly review the applications and handle the shortlisting on your behalf. Use a spreadsheet. From now on, when you see a table, it calls for a spreadsheet. See sample table below:

Table 2: Objective Criteria Scoresheet

	Table 2: Sales Person	Score
1	Minimum Diploma in Business/Sales/Engineering	1
2	Driver's License	1
3	Minimum 5 years in the Same/Related industry	5
4	Salary $5,000 per month, Commission, Benefits	1
	Total Score	8

Notice that for 5 years of experience, a score of 5 assigned. If a person has less than 5 years, say 3 years—give him a 3. But if the applicant has 5 or more years—give him a 5.

The maximum score anyone can receive is 8 and that will also be the cut-off point for shortlisting candidates.

With regards to salary, if someone indicates a higher asking pay, he gets a zero. You only want people who can accept your salary—at least, the fixed portion of their total wages.

Author's Note: Ordinarily, I'll not shortlist candidates who demand a higher fixed salary as I jealously guard my fixed recurring overheads. With the flexible element—commissions—I'm open to negotiation. But that's me. You might have your own take on it.

2.2 Recruit a Pool of Candidates

Recruit a pool of candidates and remember the larger the pool, the greater the choice. This is the class from which you're going to choose the best.

There are various avenues for recruiting: advertisements, referrals and, internal recruitments. Increasingly, organizations outsource recruitment to professional agencies who will provide a shortlist.

Assuming you are handling the recruitment, list the candidates as in the table below. For a sample, we've listed 4 people.

Table 3: Candidate List

	Table 3: Sales Person	Score	Andy	Betty	Cole	Holt
1	Minimum Diploma in Business/Sales/Engineering	1				
2	Driver's License	1				
3	Minimum 5 years in the Same/Related industry	5				
4	Salary $5,000 per month, Commission, Benefits	1				
	Total Score	8				

2.3 Short List the Candidates

The third step is to short list the recruited candidates by assigning the grades. Scan the applications and plug the grades into the table. See Table 4 on the next page.

Table 4: Shortlisted Candidates

Table 4: Sales Person	Score	Andy	Betty	Cole	Holt
1 Minimum Diploma in Business/Sales/Engineering	1	1	1	1	1
2 Driver's License	1	1	1	1	1
3 Minimum 5 years in the Same/Related industry	5	3	5	4	5
4 Salary $5,000 per month, Commission, Benefits	1	1	1	1	1
Total Score	8	6	8	7	8

Notice that Betty and Holt meet your minimum requirement of 8 points. They come onto your shortlist.

Andy and Cole at 6 and 7 points respectively do not meet your minimum requirements and are dropped.

What if none of the candidates meet your minimum requirements?

Well, you'll have to restart your recruitment. Perhaps you can try widening the net by increasing the salary offer and/or reducing the minimum years of experience.

You have shortlisted the candidates or the employment agency you engaged has forwarded a shortlist of candidates for interview.

This is where you, as the hiring manager, encounter the biggest challenges. With interviews, in most cases you've less than an hour to assess the candidate.

You might carry out the first interview and schedule a second interview together with the requesting line manager (the manager the applicant will be reporting to). Quite often, there is only one interview with both the hiring manager and line manager sitting in.

When a candidate walks in, what do you do? You ask questions and evaluate their responses. What questions do you ask and how do you evaluate the responses?

This is where the Human Capital Model kicks in.

###

Chapter 3: Types of Questions

How are questions classified? There are two broad classifications which can be labelled as:

- Question Nomenclature Classification
- Human Attribute Classification

One: Question Nomenclature Classification

Questions classified by how they are constructed:

1. Close-ended questions
2. Open-ended questions
3. Situation or scenario based questions

3.1 Close-ended Questions

These questions seek specific information and can even elicit Yes or No type answers.

Some examples:

- How many years have you been driving and have you ever been involved in a motor accident?
- In your current job, what is the value of the sales budget you are directly responsible for?

- In your current job, what percentage of your customers are multinationals, government agencies and small & medium enterprises?

3.2 Open-ended Questions

These questions go broad and might even seem unrelated to the job scope and job requirements.

Some examples:

- How do you juggle family responsibilities and job demands?

- Talk about the most difficult account you brought on board.

- How do you see yourself contributing to the business?

3.3 Scenario based Questions

These are hybrids of close and open ended questions.

They are open but with clear boundaries; and also seek specific information and cannot be replied with Yes or No type answers.

Some examples:

- You want to introduce a new product to the market, how would you go about it? Give an overview of your approach.

- Who do you see as major competitors for our products and what are their strengths and weaknesses?

- Going forward, what do you consider the biggest challenge to our industry and how would you respond?

Two: Human Attribute Classification

The classification seeks to group questions according to human traits (such as soft skills) and expertise (hard skills).

1. Questions that prompt Self-Evaluation

2. Questions that seek Promises

3. Questions that seek to Predict Behaviour

3.4 Questions that prompt Self-Evaluation

These questions require the candidate to speak of himself. They seek to uncover <u>strengths and weaknesses.</u>

Some examples:

- Speak of your strengths.

- Speak of your weaknesses.

- How will someone close to you, for example your spouse, describe you?

3.5 Questions that seek Promises

These questions try to gauge the ability and willingness of the candidate to make commitments.

Some examples:

- Why should we offer you the job?

- How do you see yourself fitting in the team?

- Where do you see yourself in five years' time?

3.6 Questions that seek to Predict Behaviour

The interviewer poses scenario questions to gauge the candidate's responses to a given situation. These responses are taken as predictive of how that candidate will respond in the future.

Some examples:

- A corporate customer is a bully but he is also a major account. How would you handle the situation?

- One of your co-worker's incompetence adversely affects your work. How would you manage the situation?

- You secured a large order and your boss has publicly praised your achievement before a gathering of your peers. When invited to say a few words, how would you respond?

As you can deduce, both classifications overlap. Questions on self-evaluation and promises can be close and open ended. And questions that seek to predict behaviour are similar to scenario based questions.

The first, nomenclature classification, focuses on question construction. The second, human attribute classification, focuses on outcomes.

It is better to focus on the outcomes: questions must have specific goals. Whenever you construct a question, remain focussed on what you hope to achieve with that question. This is crucial as in most interviews, we seek to uncover technical expertise and the intangible qualities that make up human capital.

Recap from Chapter 1, the elements of Human Capital

- Hard skills (training and qualifications)

- Technical expertise (includes experience)

- Intangible qualities (soft skills)

The hard skills are quite easily verified. They are employed to shortlist candidates.

Tenure, years on the job or popularly known as experience, is quite often mistaken for expertise. The scenario based predictive questions tend to uncover true expertise, instead of mere years on the job.

With regards to intangible qualities, which is better—integrity or loyalty? Detail oriented or hardworking? How do you consistently compare apples to oranges?

Focus on the outcome you desire, and work backwards to construct the questions. For this reason, in this handbook we shall use the human attribute classification. Don't fret over it because in reality you can construct the question and assess whether it meets your requirement. The former makes it faster. The latter—well, you'll get there.

3.7 A Mind Exercise

Before we plunge into constructing the HC Growth Model, a small detour on how our mind processes information. This would help us understand why small and medium enterprises (SMEs) can grow their Team Human Capital (THC) faster.

1. Look at this pair of numbers: 1734689876 and 1734869786.

2. Now, look at this pair: 1,000 and 1,000,000.

3. Cover the numbers—do not peek.

4. Which is the larger number in the first pair? The first or the second—do not peek.

5. Which is the larger number in the second pair, the first or the second number?

Check the answers.

If you got both answers right, congratulate yourself. You are exceptional! If you got the first wrong but the second right—no worries.

This was merely to illustrate how our mind processes information.

The wider the disparity, the easier it is to grasp the differences. The closer the differences, the more difficult it is to recognize them.

Keep this in mind as it is important when building your HC Growth Model. And this is why you need to quantify the intangible elements that make up an individual's human capital. Quantify the measure to two decimal points.

How do you utilize the various questions and approaches to assess a candidate?

The Human Capital Growth Model reveals the methodology.

Okay, enough already with the boring stuff.

Let's build the HC Growth Model—one that you can customise to suit your particular management style, corporate values, and business cycle.

Here is an overview of the 5 steps:

- **Step One**: List the Attributes
- **Step Two**: Rank the Attributes
- **Step Three**: Assign Weights to Attributes
- **Step Four**: Construct Questions
- **Step Five**: Interview and Assign the Grades

###

Chapter 4: Step One – List the Attributes

The first step, make a list of three to five attributes or soft skills that you want your staff, your team, to possess. You can make a longer list but in later chapters, you will know why it's better to keep it at three to five.

If you do not already have a set of solid attributes, brainstorm and come up with a list.

You need to identify what makes your business unique. The hints are all around the organization.

4.1 Pointers for determining Attributes:

1. What does your organization excel in; which areas do you need improvement?

2. In which areas do your competitors excel?

3. What do your customers demand?

4. As an organization, how do you hope to reach the next level of competence?

5. What is your mission statement?

4.2 Who determines the Attributes?

If you are the sole proprietor of a micro business, you decide. They're your values. Put your imprint on the business.

If you rely on several key decision makers—managers—even if you're the business owner, take a more consultative approach.

Gather and involve the internal stakeholders for their input: peers, superiors, and subordinates.

4.3 Sample Attributes

Let's assume you decided on the following employee attributes.

Table 5: Raw List

Table 5: Raw List
Hard Worker
Team Player
Adaptable
Problem Solver
Leader

By the way, you have started to customise your Human Capital Growth Model, because not every organization will select these same five attributes.

Moving on, these are the qualities you want for your team-members. Key this list into a spreadsheet.

As you develop the model, with more discussions you might wish to change the list. Do it. You can keep changing the list as long as you're in the design stage.

For now, the next step is to rank the attributes in the order of your preference. More customization.

###

Chapter 5: Step Two – Rank the Attributes

In the previous chapter, we randomly listed five attributes.

The next step is to rank the attributes in the order of importance as you see them.

Again, unless you're a sole proprietor and literally running a one-manager business, this exercise ought to be consensual and you need to get all the internal stakeholders involved—the same people who helped develop the initial random list.

You might consider one attribute more important than another. Again, quite often this depends on your preference; your place in the business cycle, such as start-up phase, growth or maturity; or even on the type of business activity.

Some examples:

- In a production line or process type of activity, you might consider Hard Worker as more important than Adaptable.

- In the creative industry such as drama productions, or in a start-up phase, where activities are more unstructured, Adaptable commands a premium.

- In the service industry, it could be Problem Solver and Team Player.

There are no hard and fast rules. You decide as you see fit. You decide on what works for your particular situation. You customize.

Let's assume you decided on the following ranking.

Table 6: Ranked Attribute List

Table 6: Ranked List	
ATTRIBUTES	Rank
Problem Solver	1
Team Player	2
Leader	3
Adaptable	4
Hardworker	5

Not only are the attributes customized, you also customized the ranking to meet your management style, business phase, and corporate values and culture.

Compare Table 6 with the unranked (raw) listing in Chapter 4. Table 5.

Think of your team as a sprint team or a swim team training hard to improve their time. But instead of time and medals, you plan to grow your human capital and profits.

That's the goal of the Human Capital Growth Model—to grow your human capital.

To run or swim faster, you need to know the time to beat.

Similarly, to grow your capital, you need to know your starting point—your current human capital.

You already have the attributes. Next, we'll measure them.

Yes, measure them like in weights and balance, and numbers. In fact, we'll actually assign weightage to the attributes.

###

Chapter 6: Step Three – Assign Weights to Attributes

Why is it important to assign <u>weights</u> or <u>weightage</u> to the ranked attributes? After all, when shortlisting job applicants (Chapter 2) we assigned unweighted grades.

Well, that worked because we were not comparing apples to oranges. We were merely grading applicants based on yes-no type questions. Here is an extract of the table from Chapter 2.

Table 7: Extract from Table 2, Chapter 2

	Table 7: Sales Person	Score	Andy
1	Minimum Diploma in Business/Sales/Engineering	1	1
2	Driver's License	1	1
3	Minimum 5 years in the Same/Related industry	5	3
4	Salary $5,000 per month, Commission, Benefits	1	1
	Total Score	8	6

- Does Andy have a diploma? Yes, he receives 1.

- Does he have a driver's license? Yes, another score of 1.

- Minimum 5 years? No, he evidently has only 3 years and therefore receives a score of 3.

- Will he settle for a $5,000 salary? Yes, again a score of 1.

Unfortunately, Andy's total score is 6 which falls below the minimum requirement of 8 points. He is not shortlisted.

Now, let's see what happens when we follow that same technique, i.e. without the benefit of weightage.

- Interview your existing staff, pose questions, and assign grades based on their responses.

6.1 Why Interview Current Staff?

We need to set the baseline, a comparator.

- The Goal: Once we established our current human capital, we employ people who are comparable or better than our existing team members. That's how we grow our Team Human Capital (THC).

6.2 What Questions Do We Ask?

In Chapter 3 we already have sample questions. In later chapters, we'll spend some considerable time developing more questions.

But for now let's assume we've a ready bank of questions.

6.3 How and What Scores Do We Employ?

We use the numbers 1 to 10, with 10 being the best or highest score and 1 for the lowest. As the candidates (or in this case, our existing staff) respond to questions, we grade them as 1 to 10.

Is this method not subjective? Yes, but as we develop the HC Growth Model, it'll self-moderate.

For now, based on the questions, assign scores one to ten. As this is only a dry run, simply assign any number between one and ten.

6.4 Enter the Scores in the Spreadsheet

1. List the names of candidates (for example) Esther, Vincent, and Jenny; the ranked attributes; and the assigned scores.

2. Interview the staff individually; treat this exercise as if it were a regular interview of job applicants. To prevent the earlier interviewees from revealing the questions, keep them separated from those waiting their turns. Do not allow access to cell phones or any other forms of communications.

3. Pose the same questions on Problem Solver to Esther, Vincent, and Jenny.

4. Depending on their responses, grade them one to ten.

5. Next, pose questions on Team Player and grade them.

6. Continue with all the questions and assign the grades.

Let's assume the interviews are complete. The table below is a typical representation.

Table 8: Raw Un-weighted Scores

Table 8: Raw (Unweighted) Scores				
ATTRIBUTES	Rank	Esther	Vincent	Jenny
Problem Solver	1	6	8	4
Team Player	2	4	5	5
Leader	3	6	6	5
Adaptable	4	5	7	6
Hardworker	5	3	3	4
Total Raw Scores		24	29	24

Notice that Esther and Jenny scored 24 points.

This does not mean they bring to the table equal compositions of attributes. Esther scored six for Problem Solver and Jenny scored four. Take a moment to study the table.

You know that Esther's score of six for Problem Solver is more valuable than, for example, Jenny's score of six for Adaptable because Problem Solver is higher up the attribute ranks.

The Raw (Unweighted) Scores do not reveal values. Look at it this way. Six kilograms of Gold is worth more (has more value) than six kilograms of Silver. To secure values, relative to one another, we need to assign weights.

The attributes that staff bring to the job are their contribution to our team's human capital. And to measure (value) the <u>amount</u> of their contribution, we assign weights to the attributes.

How do we assign weights to the attributes?

6.5 Assign Weights as Proxies for Value.

This is borrowed from Multi Attribute Analysis (MAA), a branch of Management Science. There are many fine books on MAA theory but as ours is a handbook, we'll cut to the chase.

Table 9: Attributes and Rank

Table 9: Attributes & Rank	
ATTRIBUTES	Rank
Problem Solver	1
Team Player	2
Leader	3
Adaptable	4
Hardworker	5

(This is actually Table 6 from Chapter 5 but re-labelled to retain the number sequence.) The first column in the spreadsheet lists the attributes and the second column indicates the rank.

6.6 Calculate Inverse of the Rank

To calculate the weight, the first step is to inverse the ranks, as in the third column. Inverse, divide one by the rank, 1/R, that is: 1/1; 1/2; 1/3 and so forth.

Table 10: Calculate the Inverse of the Ranks

Table 10: Inverse Values of the Ranks		
ATTRIBUTES	Rank	1/R
Problem Solver	1	1.00
Team Player	2	0.50
Leader	3	0.33
Adaptable	4	0.25
Hardworker	5	0.20
TOTAL of INVERSES		2.28

Adjust the inverses to two decimal points, as that is all the accuracy we need. The total of the inverses derived is 2.28.

Note: Instead of using a calculator, embed the formula in the cells of the spreadsheet and it'll spill out the computations.

For 5 attributes, we'll get 2.28. Column 3, last row.

With a longer or shorter list of attributes, that total sum changes. We'll cover the disadvantages of long lists a little later in this chapter.

6.7 Derive Attribute Weights

Divide the inverse by the Total of Inverses to derive the weight.

Table 11: Attribute Weights Computation

Table 11: Derive Attribute Weights			
ATTRIBUTES	Rank	1/R	Weight
Problem Solver	1	1.00	0.44
Team Player	2	0.50	0.22
Leader	3	0.33	0.15
Adaptable	4	0.25	0.11
Hardworker	5	0.20	0.09
TOTALS		2.28	1.00

- One divide by 2.28 equals 0.44

- 0.50 divide by 2.28 equals 0.22

- 0.33 divide by 2.28 equals 0.15 (rounded to 2 decimals)

- 0.25 divide by 2.28 equals 0.11

- 0.20 divide by 2.28 equals 0.09

6.8 Pointers on Weights and Number of Attributes

1. The total of the weights will always be ONE (last column, bottom right, rounded to 2 decimal points).

If it is more or less, please recheck and ensure you have rounded all weights to 2 decimals.

2. Diminishing values

In addition, notice that the weight for the first ranked attribute is 0.44. By the time we get down to the fifth rank, the weight is 0.09.

If we used ten attributes and calculated the inverses and weights, the first attribute weight would drop to 0.34 and the tenth would have a weight of a mere 0.03. (*Try it if you wish.*)

This is one reason why we keep the attribute list to no more than five. The longer the list, the tinier the weightage and the lower ranked items make very little impact.

We require only up to five attributes. Ultimately, we become best in class for that set of attributes.

6.9 Multiply Raw Score by Weight to derive Weighted Scores

Next, let's re-look the scores—this time weighted—of Esther, Vincent, and Jenny.

Be aware that when you use embedded spreadsheet formulae and select the number of decimal points, rounding off kicks in. Do not worry too much about minor differences.

Table 12: Weighted Scores

Table 12: Weighted Scores								
QUALITIES	Rank	Weight	ESTHER	Score	VINCENT	Score	JENNY	Score
Problem Solver	1	0.44	6	2.63	8	3.50	4	1.75
Team Player	2	0.22	4	0.88	5	1.09	5	1.09
Leader	3	0.15	6	0.88	6	0.88	5	0.73
Adaptable	4	0.11	5	0.55	7	0.77	6	0.66
Hardworker	5	0.09	3	0.26	3	0.26	4	0.35
TOTAL Weighted Scores			24	5.19	29	6.50	24	4.58

In the case of Esther, it is as follows:

- 0.44 for Problem Solver, multiplied by raw score 6 = 2.63 weighted score.

- 0.22 for Team Player, multiplied by raw score 4 = 0.88 weighted score.

- 0.15 for Leader, multiplied by raw score 6 = 0.88 weighted score.

- 0.11 for Adaptable, multiplied by 5 = 0.55 weighted score.

- 0.09 for Hard Worker, multiplied by 3 = 0.26 weighted score.

Giving Esther a total weighted score of 5.19.

Study the table. Notice the scores for Vincent and Jenny.

6.10 Total the Weighted Scores

Esther and Jenny, who tied at a raw score of 24 points, now show total weighted scores of 5.19 and 4.58 respectively.

This is the effect of weightage. It assigns value to the unweighted score.

Esther has a raw score of 6 for Problem Solver and Jenny has a raw score of 6 for Adaptable. But because of their varying importance, as reflected in the ranking, Esther's 6 is valued at 2.63 whereas Jenny's 6 is valued at 0.66.

This is the methodology to compare apples to oranges.

Vincent, at 6.50, brings more human capital to the table.

Esther's 5.19, Jenny's 4.58, and Vincent's 6.50 are their respective Individual Human Capital.

But every business, every organization relies on team effort. Measuring and growing team human capital is our ultimate goal.

What is this company's Team Human Capital?

6.11 Calculate Current Team Human Capital

Assuming, the three people—Esther, Vincent, and Jenny—constitute our current staff strength, we calculate our team's current human capital as follows:

Simply add all three weighted scores and divide by three:

$(5.19 + 6.50 + 4.58)/3 = 5.43$

Table 13: Team Human Capital

Table 13: Team Human Capital							
QUALITIES	Weight	ESTHER	Score	VINCENT	Score	JENNY	Score
Problem Solver	0.44	6	2.63	8	3.50	4	1.75
Team Player	0.22	4	0.88	5	1.09	5	1.09
Leader	0.15	6	0.88	6	0.88	5	0.73
Adaptable	0.11	5	0.55	7	0.77	6	0.66
Hardworker	0.09	3	0.26	3	0.26	4	0.35
TOTAL Weighted Scores		24	5.19	29	6.50	24	4.58
Team Human Capital (THC) Average of Weighted Score					5.43		

That is, our Team Human Capital is 5.43 out of a possible 10. It means we've plenty of room to grow human capital.

In this particular organization, to grow our Team Human Capital, we employ candidates who achieve a score higher than 5.43. Anything less and we draw down our human capital.

This in essence is how the HC Growth Model provides a means to identify, measure, and employ, and grow our human capital—at the individual and team levels.

In this dry run we conveniently ignored the questions and simply plugged in the raw scores.

In the next chapter, Step Four in constructing the HC Growth Model, we look at formulating questions.

###

Chapter 7: Step Four – Construct Questions

Construct questions designed to trigger and draw out responses that give insights into the qualities or attributes we seek in employees.

Interviews are high stress events for candidates seeking employment, and even for staff undergoing evaluation. Interviews are very important to job candidates and interviewers <u>must</u> accord the same level of importance to the event.

7.1 Shoddy Interviews

Assessments are subjective and interviewers make matters worse:

- They pose different types of questions.

Instead, interviewers must come prepared with a specific list of questions that uncovers well defined human attributes required to accomplish the job scope for the position.

- They pose different questions.

They roll with the punches and let the interviewee's responses dictate the questions. Take charge and don't be led by candidates primed by professional career coaches.

- They ask varying numbers of questions.

With different questions taking up different amounts of the allotted time, interviewers tweak the numbers. Stick to a well-defined and planned format.

Next, how many questions and how much time should one allocate for interviewers?

7.2 Number of Interview Questions & Time Allocation

Construct 3 to 5 questions for each Attribute or Quality we wish to uncover. If we work with three attributes, employ as many as five questions per attribute. If we have five attributes, try not to go beyond three questions per attribute.

Either way, come up with a <u>maximum of 15 questions</u>.

For most interviews, one hour is adequate. If you can spend more time, that'll be great too. Your call.

7.3 Time Allocation One Hour

- The first 2 to 5 minutes are for introductions, to allow the interviewee to gather herself, and for small talk to help her relax. We do this to help lower the anxiety for the interviewee.

- The last 10 to 12 minutes are for the candidate to ask questions. Remember, as we evaluate the person, she is also sizing-up us.

- 30 minutes for our questions: 15 questions at 2 minutes per question.

- The balance 15 minutes held as slack.

7.4 Questions

We already looked at 18 sample questions in Chapter 3.

Let's look at some more questions based on the attributes listed, ranked, and weighted. To recap, these are the attributes:

- Problem Solver
- Team Player
- Leader
- Adaptable
- Hard Worker

7.5 Questions for Leader

Let's assume we're interviewing candidates for a leadership role: supervisor, team leader, manager, and so forth.

To better illustrate, let's use specific examples. Consider the position of Operations Manager in Product Distribution.

The product can be anything: industrial or consumer items, spare parts, paper products, fabrics, medical appliances, pharmaceuticals, machinery, electronics, and so forth.

This is not an entry-level or trainee position, therefore most of the candidates applying for this job would already be holding some supervisory position and be managing some direct reports.

Keep one point in mind. When it comes to question construction there is no right or wrong. What follows are suggested questions.

Note: Feel free to modify and/or employ the sample questions. Draw on your wealth of knowledge, expertise, and life experiences. This is all part of customizing your HC Growth Model.

The question we need to ask first is one that we must ask ourselves. What does the question seek to uncover? Leadership qualities.

Good. With this in mind, consider the following three questions.

- **Question 1: Talk about your staff, and what they do.**

The question seeks to identify how well John—let's give the candidate a name—knows his current direct reports and what they actually do.

We all heard said: What the job expects John to do; what his managers think John is doing; and what John is actually doing are all different.

Going back to the question, John's possible response could be:

"Well, I've 12 people working in my department which is split into 3 sections. Customer Service, Stores/Shipping, and Quality. Customer Service handles quotations and order processing. Stores/Shipping does inventory management, the pick and pack, and delivery services. Quality implements and oversees processes and is responsible for incremental improvements."

Grade the candidate's response between one to ten based on your expectations and perceptions.

Note: The key phrase here is, your expectations and perceptions.

- **Question 2: Which job functions handled by your staff are you proficient in?**

Many people start their career with a specific skill set before getting promoted to wider responsibilities. The question seeks to identify his specific skills, something that augments his leadership abilities.

His response would also help us verify what he has put in his resume. The question also helps us learn how well he knows his current job.

Some managers might be unfamiliar with what their staff do, but rely purely on financial and other management reports and tools for their decision-making. Not exactly an ideal proposition, especially for lower level supervisors.

Note: There was this case where a manager marked down his customer service expert, let us call her Jenny. This manager did not know how to work quotes. The man relied on data that indicated number of lines quoted per employee.

Jenny apparently quoted fewer line items compared to her co-workers. Therefore, he marked her down during the annual review.

Jenny's manager was unaware that her co-workers simply lifted prices off the electronic catalogue. But when a special item not in the catalogue came through, her co-workers, who looked upon Jenny as more proficient in sourcing, handed that file to her.

She would research and verify prices, and supply and demand for the new item. Then, she would source and quote. It usually took her hours of ferreting work to construct a quote.

Instead of crediting Jenny with growing the company's product line, her manager penalized her! All because he did not know what actually happened under his watch. He relied on his 'data'—in this case, the number of line items each person quoted.

Now, going back to question two, a possible response could be:

"Oh, before I became deputy manager of operations, I started as quality inspector and installed several initiatives to cut down unnecessary processes thereby increasing productivity in customer service and shipping. Management decided the Ops Manager needed a deputy to stand in during his absence. I was selected. I love the ops job and that's why I'm applying for this Ops position."

By revealing his area of expertise—in this case, quality—we know that if employed, the candidate might require some orientation in handling customers. He is good in improving processes, loves ops, but perhaps needs some training in customer contact.

Note: If you also handle HR duties, you can add to and build your training plans.

Okay, go ahead and give him a score between one and ten, based on your perceptions and expectations.

Consider a second candidate who says something along this line:

"I started as a trainee, rotated through and did one-year stints in customer service, stores/shipping and quality. I really love interacting with customers but Quality had an opening for supervisor and management offered me the job. It meant more money, so I grabbed it. Yes, I know quality pretty well but also have work experience in customer service and stores/shipping."

What does this say about this candidate? Assuming we gave this second candidate a higher score, we should not be quick to strike out the first candidate. We've yet to determine the final weighted score based on all the attributes.

- **Question 3: If you secure the job, would it be okay for us to contact your former staff for references?**

Yes, contact <u>his former staff</u>. Of course, we also contact his former boss. The candidate's boss will know him more as a subordinate.

As we're seeking a person with leadership qualities, his staff will know him better as a leader.

Ask the candidate to send through names and contact details. And contact the references *after* he has joined your organization and during the probation period. Make clear to the candidate, put it in the employment terms that confirmation is subject to, among other criteria, the results of the reference checks. If he hesitates, it says much about his claims and more.

When we call his former staff, what would they say? Let's assume the response goes something like this:

"Oh, you mean you're asking about Mr. Lee?"

Interesting, is it not, that his former staff refer to him as <u>Mister</u> Lee. What does this say?

Alternatively, the exchange could be:

"Oh, how's John? We really miss him."

"Why is that?"

"You know, he's so nice and friendly, and…"

Try a follow-on question:

"What is it about John that you do not like?"

After all, no one is perfect and one does not get results just by being "nice and friendly".

Notice we slipped in the strengths and weaknesses question here. We posed this Self-Evaluation question on the referees and not on the candidate.

The response could be:

"Well, he drives us hard but you know what, he also pays us well. In fact, last year we blew the budget but management refused to give us a bonus and John..."

Aha! We get hints of John's management style. What does this say about John?

We begin to uncover a treasure trove of information about our candidate, John. Finally, based on our values and expectations, we interpret and assign scores to the responses.

That's 3 questions on leadership.

Next, let's take as an example another quality that most employers seek—Team Player.

7.6 Questions for Team Player

Consider questions to identify Team Player, an attribute we expect of all employees in our team.

- **Question 1: Why do you like teamwork?**

Listen to what the candidate says, how he says it, and his body language. We then draw conclusions and grade him. List down his reasons, using bullet points, and ask the next question.

- **Question 2: Why do you dislike teamwork?**

These questions fall in the Self-Evaluation category. We're asking the candidate to self-evaluate regarding a specific characteristic—teamwork. What is it about teamwork that he likes and dislikes?

Cross check his reasons against the earlier bullet points on why he likes teamwork.

- **Question 3: How would you handle interpersonal problems?**

This is a Behavioural-Predictive type question.

There's one caveat. Do not ask all three questions consecutively. People are smart—obviously, we seek smart people—and will read your intentions.

We need to stagger the questions and shall cover staggering in Chapter 9.

For each quality, each attribute, fashion at least three questions. Take into consideration how a subsequent question builds upon the preceding one, and remain focused on uncovering the traits sought.

We shall see how this works when we try to uncover another attribute—Problem Solver.

In order to cover varied job skills, let's consider a different but common position in many industries: Warehouse, Shipping or Customer Service professional.

The best means to uncover a problem solver is to pose Scenario Questions.

7.7 Questions for Problem Solver

To employ problem solvers we stipulate a minimum number of years as proxy for expertise and decision-making abilities. This is a good start but one that needs testing.

When we pose scenario questions, the candidate's responses would remove any ambiguity about his experience, expertise, and problem solving skills.

These questions not only draw out the intangibles but also verify the objective criteria—minimum years of experience, which we used as a proxy to shortlist the candidate.

7.8 Who sets Scenario Questions?

If you're a HR manager seeking someone for a HR function, you know the questions to formulate that focus on problem solving skills. You have the job specific skills to pull this off.

But if the scenario question is specific to a line function, then, we must invite that line manager to construct the questions. He knows best the problems and the kind of help he needs.

Caveat: Do not allow line managers to waste the interview session by having them cover questions which the HR person can handle. Questions such as: what is your strength; what is your weakness; and similar generic themes?

In fact, when the HR manager or hiring manager is interviewing the candidate, the line manager should keep silent; study the candidate's body language; and pick up hints regarding his character.

Where our intention is to discover Problem Solvers, questions from the line manager should focus on uncovering problem solving skills; soft skills that draw from his hard skills set.

In later chapters, we shall cover how to incorporate professional competencies or hard skills expected from say, mechanics, accountants, marketers, or other blue or white-collar positions.

7.9 Scenario Questions

But for now, let's get on with the Scenario Questions.

- **Question 1: We're a distributor. You're the warehousing, shipping or customer service manager (as the case may be). Your customer in Vietnam ordered 10 widgets. You organized a drop shipment,**

from your principal in America, to Vietnam. Your customer in Vietnam claims he received only 9 widgets. How would you resolve?

The first thing we need to remember: do not prompt the candidate. Many people can answer any open ended question when prompted, as our prompts actually give them hints regarding our expectations.

The scenario is deliberately open-ended and even somewhat vague in details. Let's consider what the candidates might say.

Candidate Allen:

"One, I will check with the Americans to verify that they shipped out 10 widgets. Beyond checking their documentation, I will insist they do a physical inventory check. Two, if they confirm having shipped out 10 widgets, I will revert to the Vietnamese and ask them to recheck their end. Three, if the need arises, I will either issue a credit note for the short-shipped widget or organize a replacement shipment."

The HR manager might consider this a pretty good answer. But a line manager would know better. That's why he needs to formulate the question and sit in the interview. Is this the best answer? How would you score this response?

Candidate Beatrice:

She said all that which Allen said regarding checking with the Americans, the principal, and the Vietnamese, the customer. However, she goes on to add:

"If the value of the widget is small, I will offer a credit note to close the file on the customer side. If the value is large, I will consult my boss and suggest a replacement shipment. Moreover, I shall lodge a claim with the freight forwarder for the missing widget."

This is obviously a better response. What score would you give Beatrice?

Candidate Conner:

"First, I will check with my customer, the Vietnamese, whether the missing widget would affect their immediate production schedule or is it for their stock purposes. This will indicate how much time I have to resolve this problem.

"Second, if it is for urgent production requirements, based on the price, I will decide to organize a shipment or if it is beyond my approval limit, I will seek my immediate supervisor's approval to effect a replacement shipment.

"Third, if it is for stocking purposes and the value is low, I might offer a credit note to close the file. But if it is a high value item, I will not offer a credit note as it will affect our sales budget. I will offer instead to include the replacement with our next scheduled shipment to save on shipping costs.

"Fourth, I will get the Americans to verify through a physical stock check that they did not make a short shipment.

"Assuming the Americans confirm having shipped the right quantity, I will next check previous shipments of widgets to Vietnam or even to other customers. I will scrutinize the shipping documents for weight and quantity. Assuming the previous shipment of 10 widgets weighed 10 kilos, and if this Vietnam shipment shows up as only 9 kilos, it indicates the Americans could have made an error.

"I will approach the Americans with this evidence. It then becomes their responsibility to make good the discrepancy. Again, if the widget is urgently required, they will have to ship replacement for the missing widget at their cost. If not urgent, they can consolidate with the next regular shipment to save themselves some cost."

What score should we give Conner?

Map his thought process and we'll discern how he juggled various factors:

1. Conner focused on customer needs: Is the widget required urgently; how would it affect their production. He displayed customer orientation.

2. Then, he sought to cut cost for his company: If not urgent, consolidate with next shipment. He was not merely trying to make the problem go away by issuing a credit. Ultimately, all his actions would benefit his employer.

3. He sought the best outcome for all, even for the supplier who short-shipped. He focused on win-win-win outcomes.

4. He started by nailing how much time he has to resolve the problem. He considered financial approval limits. He did not throw back questions at you, the interviewer, by asking: Ah, what is the cost of the widget, what will be my approval limit and so forth. He ran with the scenario you painted and chances are he will not be one to keep knocking on your door for endless clarifications regarding instructions. He showed initiative!

5. He did consider the impact on sales based on the value of the widget and did not simply latch onto a credit note to make the problem go away. He took a helicopter view!

6. Throughout several options, he considered shipping costs: a true shipping executive. He kept an eye on the bottom line!

7. He displayed initiative by his investigative and forensic work, identified the root cause, and resolved the problem without incurring any loss to his employer. He took responsibility!

Review his response and we'll discover many more hints about this candidate's expertise, experience, and working style.

The above is an example of how line managers, who construct multifaceted questions via intelligent and real life scenarios, can provoke responses which paint comprehensive portraits of soft skills—a.k.a. human capital—that candidates bring.

- **Question 2: There's a sudden surge of orders to ship out but lack the time and labour. How would you prioritise your pick-and-pack?**

And the last question.

- **Question 3: Your job involves receiving incoming shipments from suppliers, breaking bulk where required, and delivering to internal customers within your own company. What savings would you suggest with regards to shipping boxes and packing material?**

These are classic examples of scenario-based questions. They don't test theory, and don't seek to identify elusive character traits that require expensive fanciful computer modelling.

Scenario questions go beyond the paper qualifications of exam smart people and those who boast "years of experience".

We can construct scenario questions for specific line and even staff functions. The key is to get the expert managers to contribute.

7.10 Ready Bank of Questions

Including the eighteen questions from Chapter 3 and nine more questions in this chapter, you have a ready bank of twenty seven questions to use "as is" or to modify to your requirements.

Right! In the next chapter, we'll plug the questions into the spreadsheet and finalise the basic Human Capital Growth Model.

###

Chapter 8: Step Five – Finalise the HC Growth Model

Let's put together the complete spreadsheet. Assuming, you selected the five attributes we touched on in earlier chapters, and with three questions each, this is what the completed spreadsheet for the Human Capital Growth Model would look like—see the next page.

Table 14: Completed Spreadsheet

Let's navigate the model as illustrated in the table.

1. The Top Line lists the name of the Interviewer, the Position interviewed for, and Date of Interview, and Candidate Name.

2. The first column indicates the weights. The most important attribute has the highest weightage of 0.44 or 44 percent out of a total composition of 100 percent.

3. The second column lists the attributes in the order of importance as we listed them.

4. Then comes the question numbers: 1.1, 1.2, 1.3 and so forth. Take note as this is important. We will come back to this later.

5. Next column, the questions pertaining to the attributes. These samples are for illustration only. You should develop your own.

6. The last column indicates the candidate's scores.

7. We derive the Raw Score by taking the average of the three individual scores.

In our examples, we used three questions for each attribute. If you used five questions, take the average of five.

Table 14: Human Capital Growth Model - Completed Spreadsheet				
Interviewer: Name		Position Open: Customer Service Exec Date: Today Candidate Name: Alan		
WT	Qualities	No.	Questions	Score
0.44	Problem	1.1	Scenario One	4
	Solver	1.2	Scenario Two	7
		1.3	Scenario Three	10
			Raw Score (Average of 3)	7.00
			Weighted Score (Raw Score x 0.44)	3.08
0.22	Team	2.1	What is it about Teamwork that you like.	5
	Player	2.2	What is it about Teamwork that you dislike.	7
		2.3	How do you deal with interpersonal problems?	5
			Raw Score (Average of 3)	5.67
			Weighted Score (Raw Score x 0.22)	1.25
0.15	Leader	3.1	Talk about your staff and what they do.	5
		3.2	Which job functions handled by your staff are you proficient in?	6
		3.3	If you secure the job, would it be okay for us to contact your former staff?	8
			Raw Score (Average of 3)	6.33
			Weighted Score (Raw Score x 0.15)	0.95
0.11	Adaptable	4.1	Relate one mistake you made and how you recovered the situation.	4
		4.2	Relate one success you achieved and how you replicated that success.	5
		4.3	If we offer you a position in X would you accept and how would you cope?	7
			Raw Score (Average of 3)	5.33
			Weighted Score (Raw Score x 0.11)	0.59
0.09	Hardworker	5.1	Describe a typical day after you return home.	4
		5.2	Describe a typical day in your current job.	5
		5.3	Are you pursuing any part time studies.	6
			Raw Score (Average of 3)	5.00
			Weighted Score (Raw Score x 0.09)	0.45
1.0	Total Score		Total of all Weighted Scores (Out of a possible 10) - Human Capital	6.31

8. Each question cluster gives a weighted score. We derive this by multiplying the average Raw Score with the weight – embed the formulae in the cells.

9. Total the Weighted Scores to derive this candidate's Human Capital. Last row, bottom right.

Alan scores 6.31 out of a possible 10. That is his human capital for the given set of criteria.

Invest some time and carefully study this spreadsheet.

Let's remove all the scores and start with a blank spreadsheet. This is what it will look like:

Table 15: Grading the Candidate

As Alan responds to the questions, grade him and see how the data automatically updates in the spreadsheet—provided you built in the formulae.

			Table 15: Grading the Candidate	
WT	Qualities	No.	Questions	Alan
0.44	Problem	1.1	Scenario One	0.00
	Solver	1.2	Scenario Two	0.00
		1.3	Scenario Three	0.00
			Raw Score (Average of 3)	0.00
			Weighted Score (Raw Score x 0.44)	0.00
0.22	Team	2.1	What is it about Teamwork that you like.	0.00
	Player	2.2	What is it about Teamwork that you dislike.	0.00
		2.3	How do you deal with interpersonal problems?	0.00
			Raw Score (Average of 3)	0.00
			Weighted Score (Raw Score x 0.22)	0.00
0.15	Leader	3.1	Talk about your staff and what they do.	0.00
		3.2	Which job functions handled by your staff are you proficient in?	0.00
		3.3	If you secure the job, would it be okay for us to contact your former staff?	0.00
			Raw Score (Average of 3)	0.00
			Weighted Score (Raw Score x 0.15)	0.00
0.11	Adaptable	4.1	Relate one mistake you made and how you recovered the situation.	0.00
		4.2	Relate one success you achieved and how you replicated that success.	0.00
		4.3	If we offer you a position in X would you accept and how would you cope?	0.00
			Raw Score (Average of 3)	0.00
			Weighted Score (Raw Score x 0.11)	0.00
0.09	Hardworker	5.1	Describe a typical day after you return home.	0.00
		5.2	Describe a typical day in your current job.	0.00
		5.3	Are you pursuing any part time studies.	0.00
			Raw Score (Average of 3)	0.00
			Weighted Score (Raw Score x 0.09)	0.00
1.0	Total Score		Total of all Weighted Scores (Out of a possible 10) - Human Capital	0.00

8.1 No Distractions

The automatic updates by the spreadsheet allow us to give full attention to the candidate, observing his body language, the tone of his voice, the choice of words he uses—anything to help decide the score we want to give him.

Keep note taking to the minimum. Note taking diverts our attention and distracts the candidate.

Pay attention to the candidate, key in the grades, and pose the next question.

8.2 Minimize Subjectivity

By taking the average of the three questions assigned to each attribute, we moderate the scores—moderate our bias.

If there are two or more interviewers, take the average scores of all the interviewers—further moderating the subjectivity.

We shall touch on this some more in the next chapter.

8.3 A working Model

Meanwhile, guess what! Congratulations!

We now have a working Human Capital Growth Model.

This is a basic model that we can use to determine Individual and Team Human Capital.

Remember, we can add as many scenario questions and attributes as we wish.

- One, get the right average for the raw score.

- Two, be aware of diminishing returns.

Take a short break. Better yet—study Table 15. See how the table condenses everything we discussed.

It would be difficult to find a Human Capital Growth Model that beats this simplicity.

In the next chapter, we will cover tips for efficiently employing our HC Growth Model.

###

Chapter 9: Tips on Maximizing the HC Growth Model

This chapter covers some tips to get the most out of the HC Growth Model as condensed in the spreadsheet.

9.1 One Candidate per Score Sheet

Do not add columns to include all the candidates, as shown in the right of Table 16 below. Have only one candidate per sheet. This reduces the chances of the first candidate's scores affecting the subsequent candidate's scores.

Table 16: One Candidate per Score Sheet

			Table 16: Do Not Add Columns for all the Candidates			
WT	Qualities	No.	Questions	Alan	Betsy	Cathy
0.44	Problem	1.1	Scenario One	0.00	.00	0.0
	Solver	1.2	Scenario Two	0.00	0	0
		1.3	Scenario Three	0.00	0	0
			Raw Score (Average of 3)	0.00	0.0	.00
			Weighted Score (Raw Score x 0.44)	0.00	0.00	0.00
0.22	Team	2.1	What is it about Teamwork that you like.	0.00	0.0	0.00
	Player	2.2	What is it about Teamwork that you dislike.	0.00	0.	00
		2.3	How do you deal with interpersonal problems?	0.00	0	0
			Raw Score (Average of 3)	0.00	00	0.
			Weighted Score (Raw Score x 0.22)	0.00	0.00	0.0

It's no use employing the best of the candidates as the "best" in the group might not be as good as any of the people you already have on board. If at all, and as we're seeking to grow our team human capital, we should be judging against our existing staff.

Note: If you disagree. Okay. List all the candidates in the columns on the R/H and go for it. Frankly, there's no right or wrong answer to this question.

9.2 Stagger the Questions

In Chapter 7, we mentioned staggering. How do you stagger questions?

Let's review an extract of Table 15 from Chapter 8, as listed below:

Table 17: Staggering the Questions

Refer to the attribute, Team Player, as an example.

WT	Qualities	No.	Questions	Alan
			Table 17: Grading the Candidate	
0.44	Problem	1.1	Scenario One	0.00
	Solver	1.2	Scenario Two	0.00
		1.3	Scenario Three	0.00
			Raw Score (Average of 3)	0.00
			Weighted Score (Raw Score x 0.44)	0.00
0.22	Team	2.1	What is it about Teamwork that you like?	0.00
	Player	2.2	What is it about Teamwork that you dislike?	0.00
		2.3	How do you deal with interpersonal problems?	0.00
			Raw Score (Average of 3)	0.00
			Weighted Score (Raw Score x 0.22)	0.00
0.15	Leader	3.1	Talk about your staff and what they do.	0.00
		3.2	Which job functions handled by your staff are you proficient in?	0.00
		3.3	If you secure the job, would it be okay for us to contact your former staff?	0.00
			Raw Score (Average of 3)	0.00
			Weighted Score (Raw Score x 0.15)	0.00

Do not pose the questions in a consecutive manner as in 2.1, 2.2, and 2.3. When we do that, candidates might latch onto your intent.

Look at the attribute, Team Player again.

When we ask the candidate 'what do you like', and immediately follow it with 'what do you dislike'—we're prompting them.

Our focus should be to draw out genuine and spontaneous responses.

Sequence the questions as follow:

1. Start with question 1.1, move to 2.1, then onto to 3.1, and so forth, switching from one attribute to another.

This keeps the candidates on their toes and draws out answers closest to what they subscribe.

2. Once you have gone down the list, start from the top and continue with 1.2, 2.2, and 3.2, and so forth.

If for whatever reason we run out of time, at the very least we would have covered all the attributes with at least two questions.

9.3 Time and Number of Questions

Ordinarily we should not run out of time. But if we do, and managed to cover only two out of three questions—average the Raw Score by two, as the default in the spreadsheet is set to divide by three.

Better yet, extend the interview time and complete all the questions.

9.4 Number of Interviewers

Have a minimum of two interviewers: the HR Manager and the Line Manager.

You can also have a panel of three people, as multiple interviewers bring different perspectives and help moderate one another's subjectivity.

As the interview progresses, each interviewer enters their scores in their laptops. Resist the temptation to deviate from the script.

If during the progress of the interview, anyone feels the questions or their sequence need tweaking—save it till the next round of interviews. To be fair to all the candidates, do not change horses in mid-stream.

After the interviews are complete, consolidate them into a spreadsheet. We then derive the Individual Human Capital (IHC) of the candidates.

Table 18: Consolidated Score Sheet for Candidates

Table 18: Consolidated Weighted Scores - Individual Human Capital			
Interviewers	**Alan**	**Betsy**	**Cathy**
Interviewer One Weighted Score	5.99	5.44	8.00
Interviewer Two Weighted Score	6.31	6.71	7.43
Interviewer Three Weighted Score	5.50	7.11	6.90
Average of 3 Weighted Scores	**5.93**	**6.42**	**7.44**
Position Applied for: Customer Service Executive			
Date of Interview: Today			

In our example, we've three interviewers: Interviewer One, Two, and Three. Take the average of the weighted scores given by the interviewers.

In this particular interview exercise, Cathy scored the highest and you would select her for the job.

If Betsy and Alan achieved IHC higher than the team's THC, it might be worthwhile to employ them. But, if there is only one spot to fill, keep these two people in your short-list for future openings.

There you have it. A means to compare apples to oranges, and avoiding the lemons.

(But just so we're clear: lemons too have their uses—if you're making lemonade, lemon cakes, and lemon…)

In the next chapter, we touch on customizing the HC Growth Model.

###

Chapter 10: Customize at Department Level

The scenario based questions we discussed to identify the attribute Problem Solver is relevant for many customer relationship positions.

Taken in a broader context, problem solving skills are relevant to all jobs and positions—when dealing with customers, both external and internal.

It's great and even crucial to have all the soft attributes such as team player, leadership, adaptability and diligence.

10.1 Specific Technical Skills

But how about specific skills required for each job? How to grow human capital for specific job categories?

The HC Growth Model can assess specific skills required for:

- Bookkeeping

- Service and repair technicians

- Market research professionals, or

- Any number of blue and white-collar positions

10.2 Proficiency Tests

Build in proficiency tests and administer these before the interview. Proficiency tests could take the form of:

- Multiple-choice questions

- Short answer questions

- Trouble-shooting charts

- Software manipulation, or

- Any other instrument we currently use for gauging proficiency

Let's assume, we've two proficiency tests for our candidates:

1. Fifty (50) multiple-choice questions (MCQ)

Assign 100 marks for the MCQ (2 marks/MCQ). For purposes of assigning grades, divide by 10.

For example, if the candidate achieves 74 marks, that translates to a 7.4 score.

2. Ten (10) short answer questions (SAQ)

Similarly, assign 100 marks to the SAQ (10 marks/SAQ).

Assuming the candidate secures 63 marks, divide by 10 and that translates into a 6.3 score.

We've translated the scores to our One-to-Ten scale.

10.3 Proficiency Tests and Scenario Questions

We can also incorporate proficiency tests into scenario questions. Some examples:

1. Trouble shooting defects in equipment and systems—for technicians and engineers.

2. Posing 'How to' questions for manipulating management and financial information systems—for finance people.

3. Interpreting charts and graphs—for analysts.

4. Developing marketing and sales plans—for marketers.

We can employ any proficiency test customised to meet the core skills required for specific jobs.

Include these proficiency tests in the table as shown.

Table 19: Proficiency Tests and Scenario Questions

Table 19: Customise the Human Capital Growth Model					
Interviewer: HRM			Position Open: Customer Service Executive		
Date: Today			Candidate: Betsy		
WT	Qualities	No.	Questions	Test	Score
0.44	Problem	1.1	Proficiency Test One (MCQ)	74	7.4
	Solver	1.2	Proficiency Test Two (SAQ)	63	6.3
		1.3	Scenario One		5
		1.4	Scenario Two		6
		1.5	Scenario Three		7
			Raw Score (Average of 5)		6.34
			Weighted Score (Raw Score x 0.44)		2.79

Add the raw scores and divide by 5, now that there are five 'questions'.

Note: Since the proficiency tests are carried out before the interview, they should not impact our interview time.

In this example, the spreadsheet threw out the weighted score of 2.79 (raw score of 6.34 multiplied by the weight 0.44).

Manipulate this cluster of questions as you wish: one proficiency test, three scenario questions; or, two proficiency tests, three scenario questions. Customize the model to your requirements.

If you do not already have ready proficiency tests and scenario questions, rope in your line managers to help develop the tests and questions.

We can also place the proficiency test as a standalone—as one of the Attributes. Instead of five attributes, we then have six. We'll see how that looks in the next table.

- Customization: that is the Human Capital Growth Model.

The HC Growth Model is flexible and fits with your requirements. It allows you to give weightage to specific skills while retaining the soft skills that make your team stand out from the competition.

Right then. In Table 20 that follows, let's review the complete Individual Human Capital Model with Proficiency Tests included.

Table 20. Individual Human Capital Model

WT	Qualities	No.	Questions	Score
	Table 20: Individual Human Capital Growth Model - Completed Spreadsheet (with Proficiency Tests)				
	Interviewer: Name Position Open: Customer Service Exec Date: Today Candidate Name: Betsy				
0.41	Proficiency	1.1	Proficiency Test One (MCQ)	7.4
	Tests	1.2	Proficiency Test Two (SAQ)	6.3
			Raw Score (Average of 2)	6.85
			Weighted Score (Raw Score x 0.41)	2.81
0.2	Problem	2.1	Scenario One	4
	Solver	2.2	Scenario Two	7
		2.3	Scenario Three	10
			Raw Score (Average of 3)	7.00
			Weighted Score (Raw Score x 0.20)	1.40
0.14	Team	3.1	What is it about Teamwork that you like.	5
	Player	3.2	What is it about Teamwork that you dislike.	7
		3.3	How do you deal with interpersonal problems?	5
			Raw Score (Average of 3)	5.67
			Weighted Score (Raw Score x 0.14)	0.79
0.1	Leader	4.1	Talk about your staff and what they do.	5
		4.2	Which job functions handled by your staff are you proficient in?	6
		4.3	If you secure the job, would it be okay for us to contact your former staff?	8
			Raw Score (Average of 3)	6.33
			Weighted Score (Raw Score x 0.15)	0.63
0.08	Adaptable	5.1	Relate one mistake you made and how you recovered the situation.	4
		5.2	Relate one success you achieved and how you replicated that success.	5
		5.3	If we offer you a position in X would you accept and how would you cope?	7
			Raw Score (Average of 3)	5.33
			Weighted Score (Raw Score x 0.11)	0.43
0.07	Hardworker	6.1	Describe a typical day after you return home.	4
		6.2	Describe a typical day in your current job.	5
		6.3	Are you pursuing any part time studies.	6
			Raw Score (Average of 3)	5.00
			Weighted Score (Raw Score x 0.09)	0.35
1.0	Total Score		Total of all Weighted Scores (Out of a possible 10) - Human Capital	6.41

Take a moment to study the table and we'll go over it in brief.

The first thing you'll notice is, there are six attributes and not five. In this example, instead of dropping one of the "soft attributes" we've retained the original five and included the proficiency tests as a standalone.

Notice we took the average of two as the raw score for Proficiency Tests.

Notice also the weightage for each attribute had dropped, for example from 0.44 to 0.41 for the first item—first column on the left. This is the diminishing effect that kicks in when we increase the number of attributes.

But the total always remains one (1)—first column bottom row.

The candidate, Betsy, secured a weighted score of 6.41 which is the Individual Human Capital she brings to the team.

If the existing Team Human Capital is less than 6.41, she will enhance the THC. If the existing THC is more than 6.41, Betsy will not qualify to join the team.

We'll discuss more of this in the next chapter.

###

Chapter 11: Size Matters

Next, we analyse the impact of individual scores on organizations small and large.

In Chapter 1, we spoke of three types of capital. To recap:

1. Regarding Financial Capital, the big boys have a clear advantage. (This is a given. The playing field is not even.)

2. Time Capital, once spent is lost. (Affects the big and small.)

3. But with Human Capital the SMEs actually have a distinct advantage. (Aha!)

The large corporations have the financial muscle to attract the best talent. But quite often the big money goes to paying the C-level executives.

When it comes to hiring people for the trenches, large corporations pay salaries similar to and sometimes even less than SMEs.

11.1 Small Organizations and Human Capital Growth

Please review Table 13 from Chapter 6, reproduced on the next page.

The company that Esther, Vincent, and Jenny worked in, had a Team Human Capital (THC) of 5.43.

QUALITIES	Weight	ESTHER	Score	VINCENT	Score	JENNY	Score
Table 13: Team Human Capital							
Problem Solver	0.44	6	2.63	8	3.50	4	1.75
Team Player	0.22	4	0.88	5	1.09	5	1.09
Leader	0.15	6	0.88	6	0.88	5	0.73
Adaptable	0.11	5	0.55	7	0.77	6	0.66
Hardworker	0.09	3	0.26	3	0.26	4	0.35
TOTAL Weighted Scores		24	5.19	29	6.50	24	4.58
Team Human Capital (THC) Average of Weighted Score						5.43	

- The 5.43 is the average, the THC, for this team of three people.

- Put another way, 5.43 multiplied by 3 gives 16.29.

This "number" (16.29) is quite useless. Why?

Obviously, a company that has a larger headcount will have a larger "number". Moreover, even when two companies have the same headcount, their attributes might differ. What's more, their job designations, job scopes, and culture will all differ from one business to another.

What this also means is: growing your human capital is growing the quality of your team. You are measuring against yourself.

But using the "number" by itself can be quite misleading because every time you add headcount, your "number" grows. This does not equate to growing your Team Human Capital.

When we average the "number" by the headcount and derive the Team Human Capital, then we have a ready comparison.

And the goal, no matter how large or small your organization, is to strive to reach a perfect 10, a Team Human Capital of 10.

Let's assume that candidate Alan, who has an individual human capital of 6.31 (see Chapter 8, Table 14), joins the team consisting of Esther, Vincent, and Jenny.

The total score for the four people, including Alan, is 16.29 + 6.31 = 22.60. When divided by 4, this gives an average or Team Human Capital of 5.65.

- The Team Human Capital has <u>grown</u> from 5.43 to 5.65.

In place of Allen let's consider another job applicant, Fanny, who has an IHC of 4.22. To begin with we'll not employ her, as her score is below the team average of 5.43.

But for our purposes, let's go through the exercise:

The total score for four people, including Fanny, is 16.29 + 4.22 = 20.51. When divided by 4, this gives an average or Team Human Capital of 5.13.

- The Team Human Capital has <u>dropped</u> from 5.43 to 5.13.

Obviously, we filter out candidates who do not add to our THC.

Note: Incidentally, we should never assume that people filtered out are 'poor quality' candidates. On the contrary, every person is a great employee but perhaps not for the attributes we seek.

We've heard of great sportsmen, perfect 10s, but they're lousy with their money and ended up broke.

- The point is: as employers and employees, we need to find the right 'fit'.

11.2 Large Organizations and Human Capital Growth

What is the situation in a larger company of say 10,000 people with a Team Human Capital of 5.50?

That gives 5.50 multiplied by 10,000 = 55,000. (Remember, this is merely a number)

When we add Alan's 6.31, we derive 55,006.31.

Divide this by 10,001—the new headcount—and the new Team Human Capital is 5.500081.

Note: Recall how the mind processes small variations in numbers (Chapter 3). It gets worse when assessing people.

The team's human capital has gone up but is hardly noticeable. If we round it off, the Team Human Capital actually remains as 5.50. No change!

Remove Alan, throw in Fanny with her score of 4.22 and go through the routine. We derive 5.499872. The change is hardly noticeable.

Compare the results with the smaller 4-person company (Esther, Vincent, Jenny plus Alan in the first example or Fanny as in the second example).

We see how difficult it is to grow human capital in large outfits. The inverse is also true. In small companies, one rotten apple can bring the business down to its knees.

As stakeholders, as employees, as customers, we've all met incompetent managers in large corporations—and the civil service. We probably wondered how these incompetents managed to stay below the radar and coast along year after year.

Well, look at the score 5.499872 after Fanny joins the corporation.

Round it down and we get 5.50. Again, no change!

From a number crunching point of view—and modern management relies heavily on data—top management will never spot the incompetents as long as these people do not rock the boat.

- We heard the cliché: he who does nothing, makes no mistakes.

SMEs can grow their human capital faster than larger corporations. Obviously, as the smaller companies grow in headcount, the impact of every additional employee diminishes.

The smaller the organization, the greater the impact—positive or negative—of every headcount. The larger the organization, the lesser the impact from every additional headcount.

Nevertheless, organizations which consistently grow their human capital—even if each addition gives only a miniscule increase in Team Human Capital—will ultimately build best-in-class teams.

We compete with ourselves, improving the quality of our people, and our team.

We're almost done.

###

Chapter 12: Review and Conclusion

In 5 simple and easily executed steps, the Human Capital Growth Model provides a means to measure tangible and intangible qualities that welds people into best-in-class teams.

- Step One: List 3 to 5 attributes that you desire or reflects your management style, business needs, and corporate culture.

- Step Two: Rank these attributes in the order of importance as you view them.

- Step Three: Assign weights to these attributes.

- Step Four: Construct questions, specific scenario situations, and proficiency tests.

- Step Five: Interview and grade the candidates' responses.

In Chapter 9, we covered how best to extract the most benefits from our HC Growth Model.

We minimized subjectivity (the bane of interviews, selections, and assessments) throughout the process by:

1. Consensual decisions (from multiple stakeholders) regarding listing and ranking of attributes.

2. Assigning weights instead of going by 'gut feel' or 'feel good' motives.

3. Establishing a baseline with internal staff to set the comparator score.

4. Employing the same questions and methodology for all candidates.

5. Taking the average of the scores we assign to each attribute.

6. Averaging the scores from multiple interviewers.

7. Incorporating hard skill evaluation (proficiency tests).

We can customize the Human Capital Growth Model at both company and department levels—and for any type of business and job category.

Moreover, as owners and managers of small businesses we know that our hiring skills bring greater impact on our Team Human Capital. The inverse is true for larger organizations.

In Chapter 1, we set out the key takeaways:

- How much human capital an employee possesses?

- How to identify and measure an individual's human capital (IHC) and your team's human capital (THC)?

- How to acquire and grow team human capital (THC)?

Congratulations! You now have the takeaways to build your best-in-class teams.

***

If you found this book useful, please take a moment and write a short review on Amazon. I'll be grateful.

Thank you,
Eric Alagan

###

About the Author

At age 16, Eric Alagan grabbed an entry level job in the aviation industry where he learned the intricacies of cleaning toilets and making lousy coffee for mechanics. He was the youngest labourer in Singapore's fledgling aviation industry, and also the best looking. The former was a fact, and the latter was a hope. In time, he graduated to fixing airplanes and engines.

Twenty years later, he slipped into the corporate suites but kept his tool box behind his desk. It became a conversation piece—grease monkey made good. But his secret—the tool box kept him rooted. After swimming with sharks for a further twenty plus years, he retired to pursue his passion—writing.

Eric has published fiction and non-fiction books.

He is married with three adult children. Fortunately, they all take after his wife. His hobbies include road cycling, philately, and reading books. His wife of 37 years continues to love him. Like Creation, her love remains a mystery for him.

He retains his tool box—true. Continues to brew lousy coffee—also true. He is getting balder by the day, because his wife loves him. Yes, please go figure. Or pose your question in the reviews and he promises to reveal the connection between his wife's love and his balding.

###

Books by Eric Alagan

Non-Fiction:

Performance Appraisal – A Scorecard Model for Staff Evaluation
Increase F&B Sales – Secrets to Boost Profits
Property Valuation – Secrets of the Roman Decision Model

Fiction:

Beck and Call – A Business Thriller Set In Singapore
Code Shield – A Peek into Singapore's Secret Services
Mechanic Leigh – Growing Up in the 1960s (Humour)
Brothers Grinn – Humour, Parody, Satire
Grinn Brothers – Oh God, Father and More

Connect with Eric

Twitter > https://twitter.com/EricAlagan
Eric's blog for fiction > http://ericalagan.net
Eric's blog for non-fiction > https://ericalagan.co

Note: Subscribe to his non-fiction blog and gain access to FREE business tips & tutorials.

###

www.ingramcontent.com/pod-product-compliance
Lightning Source LLC
Chambersburg PA
CBHW021915190326
41519CB00008B/791